This royal throne of kings, this scept'red isle,
This earth of majesty, this seat of Mars,
This other Eden, demi-paradise,
This fortress built by Nature for herself
Against infection and the hand of war,
This happy breed of men, this little world,
This precious stone set in the silver sea,
Which serves it in the office of a wall,
Or as a moat defensive to a house,
Against the envy of less happier lands;
This blessed plot, this earth, this realm,
 this England . . .

     —*King Richard the Second*, II, 1.

York Cathedral   *Clare Leighton*

THIS REALM, THIS ENGLAND...

The Citadel of a Valiant Race
Portrayed by its Greatest Etchers

Designed and Edited by
SAMUEL CHAMBERLAIN
Introduction by DONALD MOFFAT

HASTINGS HOUSE, *Publishers*   NEW YORK CITY

FIRST PRINTING, JUNE, 1941
SECOND PRINTING, JULY, 1941
THIRD PRINTING, DECEMBER, 1943
FOURTH PRINTING (*Revised*), APRIL, 1946

5477

Introduction

THE ENGLISHMAN'S HEART is in the land, in the fields and waters and ancient forests of the countryside itself. There his spirit comes truly alive; there, if anywhere, he feels at home, his existence justified. His sense of kinship with nature is no mere poetic fancy. It is real, a part of his bone and blood and fibre. If he is lucky enough to own a bit of England, he knows his piece of land intimately and cares for it—each shrub and tree and growing thing, and the creatures that live on it and share it with him. In his inarticulate soul he finds no ready expression for such sentiments, wherefore his poets and artists have spoken for him: nowhere has British art and poetry reached nobler heights than in the interpretation of nature.

The Englishman's sentiment for the country is quite different from the tolerant, familiar affection he feels for his cities. Cities to him are mere necessities of existence, the workshops in which he earns his living; places to avoid, and to get out of as soon as the day's work is done. They are not generally beautiful except in so far as they retain, in park and garden and verdant square, artificial traces of the country. They grew by accident, unplanned—like most English things—in the fashion their people like to have them grow. The crumbling touch of time, the soft caress of ivy, lawn, and tree, the smoke of centuries, all combine to bless the town with a sense of timeless harmony which is not inherent in its architecture; and such elements of authentic beauty as it may possess—a guildhall, an old inn, or ancient manor of rose-colored brick or smoky stone—were built to satisfy not the hunger of an aesthetically minded community, but the good taste and comfortable common sense of individual citizens. That the old buildings are held in proud affection by the townspeople goes without saying. But they are loved, it is fair to add, less for their beauty than for their age, because they are—or in many cases were, alas!—familiar elements of the urban scene.

Today the English countryside is still pitted by the scars of war; many of her cities still lie in ruins. In a sense, therefore, this book can be only a memory of England—the old England that has been since the beginning of time. But in a truer sense it may be taken as a triumphant prophecy of the green and pleasant land that, when her scars are healed, will be again. Here is England, in etching, lithograph, and drawing, as her greatest artists have seen her. Stone will be set on city stone, the surface of the land will again be verdant, and her people stout-hearted in peace as they were valorous in war. Here is the England her people fought to preserve, as they fought to preserve their lives. Body and soul are one. It was worth the fight.

THE CLASSIC METHOD of defining an Englishman is to assign him a number of solid, familiar characteristics, and then to strip away, one by one, his more elusive qualities as un-English. The residue is a figure closely resembling John Bull himself—an individual whom many Americans prefer to admire from a distance. In discussing any single Englishman (who, by the way, usually turns out to be a Scot or Welshman), one is likely to reach the conclusion that although he looks like an Englishman, displays the familiar English manner, speech, and dress, he must be eternally qualified in the light of his idiosyncrasies. It is easy to generalize, to say that the British have character, the French intelligence, and that the Germans, possessing neither, have had to fall back on mechanical thoroughness; but it is never quite true. John Bull is not a typical Briton: he is a residuum.

No people have so many superficial traits in common, or seem to conform so closely to a type. Why is it then that every Englishman you meet turns out to be an exception? He is a paradox. He is also a compromise, the product of heredity, environment, and sheer accident. But with a difference: living and breeding in the seclusion of his island home for nearly a thousand years, the stream of his blood has long since left the mingled rapids of its source for the pools and quiet eddies of the plain, where it has spread out into the integrated body which, for want of a more precise term, we call a race.

That is why you can always tell a Britisher. He belongs to a separate race which was mixed and set aside to cool a thousand years ago. From his Saxon blood comes his tough and ruthless tenacity; from his Celtic ancestors his deep-hidden streak of mysticism; from his Norman conquerors his tendency to a highly specialized and aristocratic individualism. The mild and misty climate of his island has also played an important part in forming his character. The English seasons merge imperceptibly one into another, the prevailing green of summer changes slowly to autumn's russet; spring comes gently, tenderly; the sky is seldom sharp and high as in America—it leans down over the land in cloudy blue and sudden shower, as Constable painted it. Even in the middle shires the sea seems always just over the brow of the next hill, so soft and salty-damp is the air. There are no sudden changes in landscape, weather, or season, no violent extremes of heat and cold. And so with the inhabitants. Both have a natural preference for understatement, an antipathy to the immoderate.

Any foreigner who has lived in England, or even briefly visited English friends, is familiar with the sensation of feeling strangely at home, yet lost in a forest of paradoxes. Nothing is consistent, not even the general obedience to form. As a visitor, during an average day in town and country, I have been charmed, maddened, soothed, irritated, delighted, bored, puzzled, amused, shocked, richly satisfied, frightened, and exalted; and at night, when I went wondering to bed, I have carried with me the conviction that the proper salt for this bird's tail has never been ground. Why? Why? Why? Why does he roll his umbrella, do without bathrooms, drive on the left, look down on the metric system, scorn the dentist, laugh at the same jokes, put up with English food (cold shape, milk pudding, boiled bacon!)—and so on and on? Ask him. He smiles in embarrassment and replies, as like as not, "We always *have* done." (Answer enough for him!) He says it apologetically, true, and with a slightly shamefaced air. Be not deceived: the apology is not for his ignorance but for yours in presuming to ask. "Why" is a word that seems to make him always a little uncomfortable. He doesn't want to know why. He never talks, and seldom thinks, about himself or his motives. He is in fact naturally averse to thinking, if his object can be gained without it. And he is more than a little indifferent to your opinion of him anyway.

How then is he made, what makes him tick and be, this typical Britisher who does not exist? Are there certain common elements that he shares with all his race? There are.

Love of freedom—that old phrase worn smooth from handling—is one of them. The Briton never utters the word, and takes for granted the thing. When he must speak of it he uses a simple paraphrase: he says he likes to be left alone to do as he pleases. Yet if man has progressed at all in the passing ages, his greatest advance has been in the field of human liberty. Englishmen have always led this fight. But make no mistake: they led it not for humanity's sake, nor to promote the rights of man, nor for any other abstract principle, but because freedom to live their own lives is as necessary to them as air and water and salt. The principle of the thing (which is the Englishman's sugar coating to the pill of necessity) emerged only after the field had been won.

Independence—liberty in shirtsleeves—is a second racial necessity. Every Englishman, figuratively speaking, needs his own garden surrounded by a wall set with broken glass for privacy, a high-backed pew in which he may worship alone, a club or pub where he may meet his own kind on equal terms. His ideal is a home of his own, preferably in the country, a trade of his own, a family of his own, a place in which he can turn his face from the world and live as he likes even though his way may be indistinguishable from that of his neighbor. In it he may indulge in any eccentricity he pleases, secure in the tradition of British tolerance of all behavior so long as the proper forms are observed. An understanding of this fact explains a good deal. Outwardly he must conform, inwardly he may be whatever he likes. And just so long as he obeys the rules and keeps from bothering his neighbor, he is free to go to the devil—or to the angels—by any road he chooses.

Hence his faith in private enterprise and his dislike of public meddling. The British Empire was invented by tough-minded, imaginative, and ambitious men like Clive and Cecil Rhodes. They and others like them opened the way, then the government stepped in and gave their enterprises retrospective sanction, gradually absorbing them into the Empire. It is said that the Empire was founded in a fit of absent-mindedness; an exaggeration, no doubt, but one that contains bits of the truth in that like most British undertakings, the initiative was supplied by private individuals.

Drake, Frobisher, Raleigh and other great Elizabethan captains set the style. Before the defeat of the Spanish Armada England was one of many minor kingdoms embroiled in European affairs through her rulers' interest in dynasties, loot, and God. Suddenly she felt a mighty wind blowing over the edge of the world, she lifted her head to meet it, and Europe was forgotten forever. Beyond the distant horizon England suddenly found her true destiny; and there has never been a moment since that she has not been in danger.

Empiricism is the philosophical theory which attributes the origin of all knowledge to experience. It is made in England. Every British institution from the Crown and the Church and Parliament down, is the product of evolution guided by practical common sense. The average Briton prefers hit-or-miss, trial-and-error methods to logical but untested theory. His institutions are designed—though never deliberately—to meet one requirement: workability; and to gain this end he will agree cheerfully to almost any kind of inconsistency or compromise. If a thing works pretty well over a long enough period it is eventually accepted as a tradition, he no longer needs to bother his head over it, and he has leisure to devote himself to the real business of living—his own affairs.

Once an institution—Parliament, for example, or the Common Law—has become a tradition, it is respected and supported by public opinion. Because the law has been justly administered in England for a very great number of years, the Englishman has become a notoriously law-abiding creature, and the tradition of honest public service part of his very marrow. The individual lives up to the responsibility imposed on him by the law because he knows by experience that with all its anachronisms and imperfections it serves him well. He sees in it an instrument devised for the protection of his rights, and over the years he gives it his duty. Not his regard, perhaps—that is reserved for the Crown, the symbol of his highest aspirations. For it he feels a deep and affectionate loyalty that has nothing to do with his personal affection for his Sovereign. That depends on how nobly the King himself has earned it.

Faith in tradition is a heritage of all the British people, little as well as great. Such a paradox is possible only because Equality, with all that the idea connotes, is to them not only an unnatural abstraction, but a falsification of Nature itself. The British concept of equality is one of the hardest things for an American to comprehend, and undoubtedly lies at the root of many of the misunderstandings between the two races. The British see no equality in nature, no essential equality in man. Our concept, they consider a purely artificial one. To them it is an aspiration, not a fact; and they take the evidence of their eyes to prove it, not of their hearts.

"The Englishman is far too much of an individualist to believe in Equality or really want it to come," wrote Paul Cohen-Portheim in his penetrating study entitled *England, the Unknown Isle*. "England is the land of the great stock-breeder and the individual prize specimen; in the same way as it breeds unsurpassed race-horses, dogs, prize cattle, roses, orchards, and peaches, it has also produced a human type, the individual produced at the expense of the masses; but being also the land of wisdom and strong humane feeling, it tries to soften and cover up excessively sharp contrasts and raise the largest possible number of the race to a higher level. . . . The Englishman wants an aristocracy; but, as a man of compromise, he wants it to have democratic features; so he created the first democracy of Europe, but based it on an aristocracy which retained its supremacy through all the centuries by constantly absorbing new blood." From where? From "below"; from the rich middle class, which in turn recruited itself from the laboring class. It is a perpetual process of natural selection of the ablest, a process based not on the abstract theory of equality, nor on any rights inherent in such a theory, but on the approval of the great majority of all classes.

One aspect of his prejudice in favor of selective breeding is the Briton's faith in character as opposed to pure intellect. He instinctively distrusts mere cleverness and "nothing but brains"—the specialist in fact. For his leaders he prefers men from whatever source (though preferably aristocratic) in whose character he feels confidence. Brains and special knowledge and ability, he believes, can always be hired or drafted in an emergency. Hence the Baldwins and Chamberlains, and the country's tolerance of them to a point almost beyond disaster. Though Churchill's background and character are not of course dissimilar, Churchill has brains and imagination too—fire and steel!—wherefore in ordinary times he was never wholly trusted. But when the crisis came, how instantly the nation recognized the need for his particular kind of inspired leadership, and how quickly he was put in command!

In the nick of time! How many, many times have the British waited till the very last moment, victims of their native faith in compromise, procrastination, and laissez-faire—then summoned their genius and, at immense and unnecessary sacrifice, got the job done. One might say of the Briton that everything in his nature conspires to get him into trouble and then, at the last possible minute, out again. His dislike of extremes, his distrust of impulse, his homely simplicity, his easy-going friendliness, his tolerance and willingness to believe the best, his aversion to planning, and to self-analysis or analysis of any kind; his reliance on experience, and on form in all the little amenities of daily life. Live and let live!

The British Commonwealth has always been as much a spiritual as a material union. The sentiment that binds it together is as strong as the bonds of self-interest. In truth, the two run together, with the unwritten accord firmer than any formal constitution or agreement could possibly make it. When, therefore, one accuses Britain of having fought merely to keep what is hers, one is guilty of a half-truth. She fought for her own, of course: Churchill spoke the truth when he said that he did not "become His Majesty's first minister in order to preside over the liquidation of the British Empire." But just as truly she fought for the idea of decency in human intercourse—decency being a British word of understatement for all the things no Briton cares to talk about, like honor.

It has been said, and by the mean-minded believed, that a little group of rich and powerful men bamboozled the Empire into the service of defending their property. If this is so, why was it the Tories who sought appeasement in 1938 and '39 and the common people who repudiated it, never hesitating in the choice between resistance and surrender? What had they to gain, these little people—underpaid cockney workers, miners living idly on the dole, slum-dwelling factory hands and small shopkeepers making a bare living from their trades? Why should they have gone cheerfully and indomitably to war? What were they fighting for? Revolution? The opportunity to upset society and drag their rulers down? No. For the right to live as free men.

There were those who predicted a new communism emerging from the chaos of war, or even a dictatorial embodiment of everything Britain fought against. How wrong these gloomy prophets proved! The fundamental bases of democracy—free speech, free assembly, a free press—are as strong today as ever they were. The Crown has survived, as much beloved as ever; and parliamentary government, and law. Many an ancient right that was suspended during the war is beginning to look alive again. Could one ever have dreamed that the abrogation of such rights were possible, when Britain had her back literally to the wall, had not every Englishman complete confidence in his ability to get them back again when the fighting ended?

The social reforms introduced by the Labour Government were predictable if not indeed inevitable. In most cases they were long overdue. But it must never be forgotten that in his private capacity, if not in his political, the average Englishman has never really cared a pin what kind of tag his government carries so long as it does the job. Call it socialism, communism, democracy, what you will: if it works in practice and assures his fundamental liberties, it is good enough for him. England has been changing in her ponderous fashion for generations. The imperative demands of war sped the process, destroyed many artificial barriers, and taught, among other things, a new kind of mutual respect among all classes. These lessons have not been lost, and will not be forgotten during the hard years that lie ahead. Today the Englishman is hungry, shabby, disillusioned, and bewildered: which side won, anyway? he well may ask. He knows the answer: Britain is free.

Britain has survived, bone-tired. Her recovery will be a slow process. But who can doubt the certainty of it, as who can doubt that the new England will be reborn in the familiar image? One need never have looked for a prefabricated post-war Utopia, drawn up to rosy specifications. Once more, as so often in her history when disaster has had her by the throat, she is digging down to the roots of her fortitude for the stuff she is made of. Slowly, deliberately, with a push here from a Royal Commission, a plan there from a civic group, and doubtless a flash of genius from some young Christopher Wren, a new Britain will arise as a new Britain rose after Cromwell's revolution, as a new London sprang from the ashes of the Great Fire nearly three hundred years ago. Though it can no longer be said of any nation that she in unconquerable, it can truly be said of the human race. Slowly, by trial and error, her favorite method, unconquerable Britain will fight her way back to the sun.

She is not a bellicose member of the family of nations. Her choice has always been to put off, to defer, to hope for an issue without decision; and when the decision can no longer be postponed, to look for some ground of compromise. But when the last hope of peace is gone—then she has always fought, as she fought for six long years, to the bitter end: fought whether or not she saw the gleam of victory ahead, fought because it is inconceivable to her that anyone who will go on fighting, and on, and on—can ever be beaten. Time means nothing. Odds mean nothing. Her refusal to accept defeat means everything. Therefore she lives unconquered.

This is the whole answer to the shameful question one heard in the black days of '39 and '40, Why did Britain fight? She fought because courage is her nature. And if it pleased her to carry her courage not like a banner but as a pocket-piece, a secret talisman, who shall grudge her the pride? In its time it has defeated many an enemy—those blind ones who, not seeing it worn like a plume in her helmet, thought therefore that she had lost it. No, she carried it through the war as she carries it now, in the inmost pocket of her heart; and its magic will always warm and lift up the hearts of mankind.

Twenty-five years ago Sir James Barrie delivered an address to the students of the ancient Scottish University of St. Andrews, on the occasion of his installation as Rector of the University—the first and only public oration of his life. His words apply to the struggle for recovery which lies ahead of Britain as surely as it does to the qualities that brought her victory in war. In simple, homely terms he spoke to them of Courage, "the lovely virtue":

"Courage is the thing. All goes if courage goes. What says our glorious Johnson of courage: 'Unless a man has that virtue he has no security for preserving any other.' We should thank our Creator three times daily for courage instead of for our bread, which, if we work, is surely the one thing we have a right to claim of Him. This courage is a proof of our immortality, greater even than gardens 'when the eve is cool.' I cannot provide you with this staff for your journey. You shall cut it—so it is ordained—every one of you for himself. It is the lovely virtue—the rib of himself that God sent down to his children. Pray for it. . . . The end will indeed have come to our courage and to us when we are afraid in dire mischance to refer the final appeal to the arbitrament of arms. I suppose all the lusty of our race, alive and dead, join hands on that.

> 'And he is dead who will not fight;
> And who dies fighting has increase.'"

DONALD MOFFAT

THIS REALM, THIS ENGLAND . . .

Contents

Piccadilly Circus, Night   *Sir Muirhead Bone*

London - The Heart of an Empire

Ludgate Hill   *William Walcot*

Somerset House   *Sir Muirhead Bone*

The Horse Guards   *Hedley Fitton*

The Monument
Joseph Pennell

Strand With Sky   *Francis Dodd*

Demolition of St. James Hall   *Sir Muirhead Bone*

1

St. James Palace—London   *Louis C. Rosenberg*

St. Paul's   *William Walker*

The Guildhall   *Joseph Pennell*

Charing Cross   *William Walcot*

Chelsea   *Charles J. Watson*

Westminster Evening   *Louis Weirter*

Trafalgar Square

The Storm—Trafalgar Square   *Rachel Carnegie*

Westminster Bridge   *Félix Buhot*

Kensington Gardens   *Sir Francis Seymour Haden*

Park Lane   *Joseph Pennell*

Kensington

Geoffrey H. Wedgwood

St. Mary Abbots, Kensington   *Louis Rosenberg*

Westminster Bridge   *James McNeill Whistler*

On the Thames—Low Tide   *Donald Shaw MacLaughlan*

London Bridge   *Joseph Pennell*

A Thames Barge off Greenwich   *Charles W. Cain*

1

The Lime-Burner   *James McNeill Whistler*

The "Adam and Eve", Old Chelsea   *James McNeill Whistler*

Billingsgate   *James McNeill Whistler*

Eagle Wharf   *James McNeill Whistler*

Hungerford Bridge   *Kerr Eby*

Tower Bridge—Evening   *Joseph Pennell*

Battersea Steamboats   *Joseph Pennell*

Kennington Lane   *Francis Dodd*

Peckham
Francis Dodd

St. George The Martyr   *Francis Dodd*

London Tower and Tower Bridge

London From The Victoria Tower

Durham   *Henry Rushbury*

Towns and Cities of England

The City of Wells   *George Marples*

The Edwards Tower—King's College Chapel—Cambridge   *William Walker*

King's Parade—Cambridge   *Raymond T. Cowern*

Stow On The Wold

Francis Dodd

The Moor—Falmouth

Sir Muirhead Bone

Leeds Warehouses   *Sir Muirhead Bone*

Founder's Tower, Magdalen College—Oxford   *Samuel Chamberlain*

Worcester

Worcester—Air View

Broad Street—Ludlow
Samuel Chamberlain

Georges Dock—Liverp
Sir Frank Short

unrise at Durham

Liverpool

The Debtors' Prison—York   *Henry Rushbury*

Polperro Harbor

Cement Works—Rochester

William Palmer Robins

Cockayne

Frederick L. M. Griggs

Hillside Town

Conway

Strolling Players At Lydd   *Sir Frank Short*

Villages

The Rising Sun—Kingston   *Sir Frank Shor*

Sunset—Cattawade   *James McBey*

Kersey

The George—Norton St. Philip

The Bridge   *Martin Hardie*

Reflections At Finchingfield   *John Taylor Arms*

Street Scene In Kersey   *Samuel Chamberlain*

Clovelly

Longstock

The Market Hall—Chipping Campden

Aston-sub-Edge · *Samuel Chamberlain*

The Almshouses—Chipping Campden

Essex Village   *Samuel Chamberlain*

Dunster

Sulgrave Manor

The Manor—Upperswell

Samuel Chamberla

Livestock Fair
Ambleside

At Crowland
Samuel Prout

1

Lynmouth

Abbotsbury Priory

Burford   *Samuel Chamberlain*

Mill Lane—Warwick

Brick Kilns—Sandwich   *Henry Rushbury*

Low Tide—Shoreham   *William Palmer Robins*

Plane Tree Cottage   *Robert S. Austin*

Farms

Priory Pond—Stroud   *S. R. Badmin*

The Weald of Kent   *Martin Hardie*

Hawes Farm—West Wickam, Kent   *S. R. Badmin*

The Quarry   *C. F. Tunnicliffe*

Priory Farm   *Frederick L. M. Griggs*

Wheatfields   *C. F. Tunnicliffe*

Martin's Hovel   *Robin Tanner*

Nichol's Farm   *Paul Drury*

A Little Black Barn in Suffolk   *Leonard Squirrel*

Duntisbourne Rouse   *Frederick L. M. Griggs*

Great Tithe Barn   A. R. Middleton Todd

A Cotswold Farm   *Henry Rushbury*

Haymaking at Elterwater

Farm on Bodmin Moor—Cornwall

A Buckinghamshire Farm

C. H. Spencer

7

Blossom Time in Kent—Sittingbourne

Early Spring   *Robert S. Austin*

Surrey Downs   James McBey

The English Countryside

Egham Lock   *Sir Francis Seymour Haden*

A Water Meadow   *Sir Francis Seymour Haden*

Rowan On The Hillside   *Walter James*

Cader Idris—North Wales   *John Sell Cotman*

In Wensleydale   *Anthony R. Barker*

Black Mill   *Frank Brangwyn*

The Ballantrae Road   *Sir Muirhead Bon*

Salisbury Plains   *Kerr Eby*

Chanctonbury Ring *Beatrice M. Christy*

Old Holly and Poacher *E. G. Earthrowl*

After A Storm—Amberley   *Malcolm Osborn*

Linse Hill   *E. Herbert Whydale*

he Northumberland Coast   *Oliver Hall*

lovers' Barrow   *E. Bouverie-Hoyton*

Spring—After John Constable

David Luc

Pecken Wood

Graham Sutherlan

Cottages and Harvesters   *Sir Frank Short*

Cross Hands   *Frederick L. M. Griggs*

Ely: Storm Coming   *Stuart Brown*

The Solent   *Sir Muirhead Bone*

lway Moss   *Sir Frank Short, after Turner*

shburnham   *J. C. Stadler*

Near Chichester   *H. F. Warin*

An English Common   *John Fullwoo*

Junction of the Severn and Wye   *J. M. W. Turner*

Dune Grasses—River Camel—Cornwall

Polperro   *Kerr Eby*

High Knaps   *E. Bouverie-Hoyton*

Swinbrook Bridge   *S. R. Badmin*

The Good Earth

Rayrigg Bay—Windermere

Lake Buttermere

Devon Reeds—Slapton

Denbighshire

The Harrow on Sussex Downs

Stonehenge

Spring Morning—Wiltshire

An Englishman's Home

A Fisherman's Cottage

Upland Plowing

Ben Lomond

Sir D. Y. Cameron

Scotland

Hills of Tulloch   *Sir D. Y. Cameron*

1

Pitman Moor   *Joseph Gray*

The Moray Firth   *James McBey*

Ben Ledi   *Sir D. Y. Cameron*

Near Glencaple on the Nith   *Sir D. Y. Cameron*

Kyleakin   *James McIntosh Patrick*

Dinnet Moor   *Sir D. Y. Cameron*

Loch Tay and Ben Lawers—Kenmore

Loch Voil

Loch Lomond

The Town of Dumbarton

Gourock   *Albany Howarth*

Tyndrum—Loch Tulla

Badenoch   *Joseph Gray*

Balmoral Castle

Scottish Hills

The Tyne   *William Walcot*

Rivers

On the Wavenay   Henry Rushbur

Walberswick Ferry—1914   Sir Muirhead Bon

Putney Church   *A. Evershed*

Sawley Abbey   *Sir Francis Seymour Haden*

Fulham on the Thames   *Sir Francis Seymour Haden*

Banks of the Thames   *Maxime Lalanne*

hepherds Pool—Orchy   *Norman Wilkinson*

he Trent   *Frederick L. M. Griggs*

River Thames—Near Cookham

The River Wye

View of the Thames at Streatly   *Robert Havell*

Millbank on the Thames   *John Sell Cotman*

Cornwall   *Sidney Tushingham*

The Coast of England

Gale at Port Errol   *James McBey*

Mersea: Sunset

James McBey

Sunset at Heybridge

Martin Hardie

Ready for Sea

Sir Muirhead Bone

126

Richborough   *Henry Rushbury*

The Mystery Ship—Padstow   *Sir Muirhead Bone*

5

Sunset on the Thames   *Sir Francis Seymour Haden*

Anchor Quay   *Francis Dodd*

The Port—Newquay   *Joseph Pennell*

Vessel in Distress off Yarmouth   *Sir Frank Short, after Turner*

Mevagissey

Mevagissey

Plymouth from the Sea

La Corbière Lighthouse—Channel Isles—Jersey

vening Near Duntulm, Coast of Skye

St. Michael's Mount—Penzance

Across Loch Var—Kasaig—Isle of Skye

Peveril Castle   *Sir Frank Short*

Castles

Richmond Castle   *Percival Gaskell*

Kilchurn Castle   *Kenneth Steel*

Carnarvon Castle   *John Sell Cotman*

Dolbadarn Castle—North Wales

John Sell Cotman

Windsor Castle

Windsor Castle from the Playground of Eton College   *Robert Havell*

Knaresborough Castle

Kenilworth Castle

Bamborough Castle   *John Sell Cotman*

The Maypole   *Frederick L. M. Griggs*

Conway Castle

Edinburgh Castle

Compton Wynyates

Hampton Court Palace

Montacute House

Madeley Court—Shropshire

Samuel Chamberlain

t. Mary's—Nottingham   *Frederick L. M. Griggs*

Churches and Cathedrals

The Five Sisters—
York Minster
Sir D. Y. Cameron

Church of St. Walburg   *Frank Brangwyn*

Night in Ely Cathedral   *James McBey*

Canterbury Cathedral   *H. Gordon Warlow*

St. Botolph's—Boston   *Frederick L. M. Griggs*

St. Ippolyts   *Frederick L. M. Griggs*

49

Stratford Church   *Fred Slocombe*

Tattershall   *Frederick L. M. Griggs*

Durham Cathedral Reflected in the River Wear

Salisbury Cathedral

The Isle of Ely   *James McBey*

Ely Cathedral

Dunfermline Abbey

Exeter Cathedral

Iona Cathedral

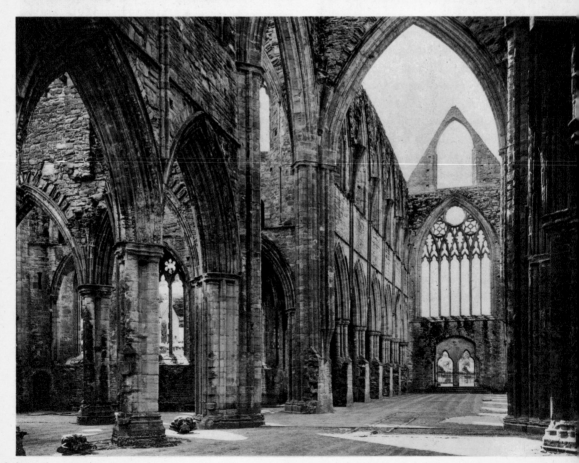

Tintern Abbey Ruins

Editor's Note

THE PRECEDING PAGES have demonstrated, I trust, that England possesses few more eloquent, loyal and sympathetic spokesmen than its graphic artists. This is not surprising, for England has been the admitted citadel of etching for generations. Today the greatest names in the art are still British, and a younger clan of talented etchers is coming along to carry on the tradition.

A composite and heart-rending picture of England as it was has been drawn here by these generations of print makers. Havell, Cotman, Lucas and Turner give a revealing glimpse of earlier and more peaceful days. Whistler, Haden, Pennell and Griggs represent the great age of etching at the turn of the century. Bone, Cameron, McBey and Short, the masters of today, make perhaps the most conspicuous contributions. And the younger generation of British etchers, many of whom are in the Services, bring the picture up to date, aided by a few prints by American etchers.

Photographs play an important part in creating a vivid picture of contemporary England, and these have been freely intermingled with the prints. The result is a convincing ensemble which, for convenience, may be divided into several categories: London, Scotland, towns and cities, villages, farms, the countryside, the coast, castles, churches and cathedrals. All of the prints and photographs have been selected with a single purpose in mind—to portray the real, living England. All of them speak eloquently for themselves,

but a few supplementary remarks about the prints and their makers may be of interest.

Sir Muirhead Bone's drypoint of PICCADILLY CIRCUS—NIGHT, an incredibly difficult subject, shows the heart of London as it looked during the first World War, with searchlights piercing an inky sky, and Piccadilly itself a far gayer place than it is during the present blackouts. Technically this is one of the most brilliant accomplishments in drypoint. The edition of this plate was sold to raise funds for war relief. William Walcot, architect-etcher and imaginative restorer of ancient Rome and Egypt, has a gift for atmospheric suggestion and a sense of huge scale which is well demonstrated in his sensitive etching of LUDGATE HILL. One can almost feel a light London fog in this busy street scene, with the immense dome of St. Paul's looming faintly in the background. The same indefinable subtlety haunts his print of CHARING CROSS, on page 22. Bone's dignified and serene SOMERSET HOUSE, one of the most sought-after of his drypoints, is an unusual composition which has been brought off successfully, due partly to the daring wiping of the sky. Hedley Fitton's large plates of picturesque European subjects, in the tradition of Axel Haig, are well known. His interpretation of THE HORSE GUARDS is dignified and direct.

America's own Joseph Pennell made innumerable sketches of London, most of which now repose in the Library of Congress. Two of these, THE MONUMENT on page 16 and

BATTERSEA STEAMBOATS on page 35, were selected for these pages. They were drawn, as were so many of Pennell's sketches, on paper with a rough linen surface. If Bone has a rival as a drypoint delineator of London, it is Francis Dodd, whose STRAND WITH SKY is as striking as it is skillful. The first printings of this plate showed a clear sky; the bold, almost Rembrandtesque tone appeared in later states.

The DEMOLITION OF ST. JAMES HALL, Bone's vivid and mightily-scaled picture of peacetime destruction, cannot help but remind one of similar scenes which occurred in the harassed capital during the bombing raids of World War II. Bone made an equally impressive exterior view of this same subject. Louis C. Rosenberg, the American etcher who is considered one of England's own by most print lovers there, contributes two skillful drypoints to this small gallery of London monuments: ST. JAMES PALACE (page 19) and the graceful spire of ST. MARY ABBOTS, KENSINGTON on page 29. William Walker's large drypoint of ST. PAUL's portrays the classic splendor of the façade in dramatic fashion, although his point of view is so close that the dome does not appear in its true proportion. The late Joseph Pennell did not foresee the fate of THE GUILDHALL when he made this free, almost impressionistic etching of it towards the turn of the century. The same unfettered freedom is noticeable in his PARK LANE on page 27. Pennell is visibly influenced by Whistler in his Thames views (pages 31 and 35), but he lacked the purity of line of the master whom he revered so highly. Weirter's striking study of WESTMINSTER EVENING is in reality a large colored etching. Félix Buhot was among the few French etchers who worked in London, and he produced one of the most celebrated etchings of the city, one

that causes a flurry in any auction room. It is WESTMINSTER BRIDGE (page 25), a busy scene enlivened with the poetic marginal sketches which were in favor in Buhot's time.

Few copper-plate renditions of trees in sunlight have been as brilliant and successful as Sir Francis Seymour Haden's KENSINGTON GARDENS, an immensely difficult subject which he has carried off with complete mastery. Never content with his laurels in the medical profession, or with the mere distinction of being Whistler's brother-in-law, Haden worked ceaselessly in the fine Rembrandt tradition of etching, and deserves to be rated as one of the great landscape etchers of the world. A Kensington of a different sort is revealed in Geoffrey H. Wedgwood's factual aquatint of rooftops and rear elevations. This artist is best known for his engravings of Italy, made while he was working as a Rome Prize winner.

One is safe in making the sweeping statement that no series of London etchings has ever excelled James McNeill Whistler's Thames set. The five examples reproduced here will give an idea of his amazing sensitiveness, his perception and delicacy of line. The only American ever to become president of the Royal Academy, Whistler repaid England for that honor with these lovely Thames etchings alone. The "ADAM AND EVE," OLD CHELSEA, is considered a turning point in Whistler's career, between the etched style of his Thames set and the more relaxed handling of the Venetian series. The late Donald Shaw MacLaughlan, another American expatriate highly esteemed in England, shows the Whistler influence strongly in his ON THE THAMES—LOW TIDE, as does Kerr Eby, whose London-grey HUNGERFORD BRIDGE is shown on page 34.

No British etcher seems to have caught the

spirit of the little-drawn suburbs of London as well as Francis Dodd. He has a peculiar gift for finding a rich composition in unexpected places; witness the animated KENNINGTON LANE on page 36. The street scene in PECKHAM could be nowhere but in England. Traffic, instead of going properly to the left, seems to be moving to the right in two of these prints, leading to the possibly mistaken surmise that the subjects were not reversed on the copper plates, and thus come out in reverse on the print.

DURHAM, by Henry Rushbury, is a capable rendition of one of England's most picturesque towns by one of her most gifted architectural etchers. Town life in England seems to be summed up in this one revealing print. A disciple of Bone, Rushbury has few equals in the handling of drypoint or in the choice of a brilliant subject. The roof of a cathedral furnishes a fine bird's-eye view of a country town, as George Marples' etching, THE CITY OF WELLS, demonstrates very well. There is a touch of Meryon in this print, attributable perhaps to the crows. The two prints on page 41 prove that collegiate Cambridge is an etchable subject. The atmosphere of a small English town on a gray day is convincingly caught in Francis Dodd's STOW ON THE WOLD, in the Cotswolds.

Sir Muirhead Bone, the supreme master of drypoint, has made pencil drawings which are acclaimed almost as highly as his prints. In World War II as well as in World War I he was commissioned by the War Office to make official drawings. The drawing of THE MOOR—FALMOUTH is a good specimen of his disarmingly direct pencil style. His ability to find a drypoint subject in unexpected places is again demonstrated in his dashing print of LEEDS WAREHOUSES. One can almost feel his needle ripping through the copper as it boldly delineates the building on the right.

Of Oxford's many towers and domes, none is more graceful than the FOUNDERS' TOWER, MAGDALEN COLLEGE, on page 44. An interesting photographic study appears on the next page, with the town of Worcester seen from the air and then from the opposite riverbank. The familiar towers of the town may be picked out in both views. The essence of all the towns of England is expressed in the timbered BROAD STREET—LUDLOW, terminating at the classic Town Hall, with the square Gothic tower of the church looming behind it. Liverpool is portrayed in two different moods on pages 46 and 47. Sir Frank Short's etching is calm, almost static—not the way one usually thinks of the great port. The photograph shows it to be sometimes radiantly exciting, bathed in a light which would do justice to the Bay of Naples.

Rushbury's dramatic sense and architectural astuteness are again demonstrated in his fine composition of THE DEBTORS' PRISON—YORK, which, at first sight, might almost be mistaken for a scene on the banks of the Tiber in Rome. Rushbury handles his blacks with masterful skill. Two contrasting moods are portrayed on page 49. William P. Robins' aquatint of the CEMENT WORKS—ROCHESTER is stark realism, whereas the fanciful COCKAYNE, by the late Frederick L. M. Griggs, is an architectural dream. Griggs, the great romanticist of etching, is at his happiest in such a mystic, mediaeval mood.

The villages of England are introduced by a heart-warming etching, STROLLING PLAYERS AT LYDD by that revered English master, the late Sir Frank Short. At the Royal College of Art he influenced generations of younger etchers. Though he was at home in any medium, as these pages show, he was at his happiest and freshest, perhaps, in the pure bitten line. Certainly his interpretation of THE RISING SUN—KINGSTON is as joyous, clear cut, and economical of line as are very few etchings. A sun of a different sort is suggested with blinding emphasis in James McBey's SUNSET—CATTAWADE. One of this master's many contributions to the vocabulary of etching is his device of indicating a setting sun by a mere blank space in his plate, a void so cleverly played up by surrounding values that it almost burns with light.

The village of Kersey, one of the most picturesque in England, is seen by the camera on page 53 and by the sketcher's pencil on page 55. The invariable square church tower dominates both scenes, as it does Martin Hardie's drypoint of THE BRIDGE. Mr. Hardie, a pupil of Sir Frank Short, is Keeper of the Engraving Department at the Victoria and Albert Museum, London. Another square tower occurs in REFLECTIONS AT FINCHINGFIELD, by John Taylor Arms, the most active individual force in American etching today. The minute and beautiful draftsmanship in this plate is lost in the reproduction. A perfect Cotswold stone cottage at ASTON-SUB-EDGE has been recorded in pencil on page 58 by this commentator, whose drypoint ESSEX VILLAGE (Newport), appears on the following page and on the jacket of this book. SULGRAVE MANOR, the home of George Washington's ancestors, and THE MANOR—UPPERSWELL are both good examples of the manor-house type that is found in so many of the hamlets of rural England. Samuel Prout, master draftsman of the 19th century, loved the sketchable aspects of English villages, as his little softground proves (page 61). William Palmer Robins might be called a modern counterpart of Prout, for his aquatint, LOW TIDE—SHOREHAM, has many of the same

fine qualities. Rushbury's sensitive drypoint of the BRICK KILNS—SANDWICH completes the village picture.

The chapter on FARMS begins and ends with plates by Robert Austin, one of the most gifted and individual of English engravers. He is equally adroit at portraiture and is, I suppose, as worthy an heir to the tradition of Albrecht Dürer as any man now living. There is an archaic charm to his PLANE TREE COTTAGE, a plate which might almost have been engraved three centuries ago. Another devoted interpreter of farm life is S. R. Badmin, whose PRIORY POND—STROUD and HAWES FARM—WEST WICKAM, KENT, show his love for texture in tree and stone. C. F. Tunnicliffe's two plates reveal an interest in the more human side of the farm. A fine solidity dominates his etchings of farm animals. In WHEATFIELDS he has caught the essence of midsummer in unforgettable fashion.

A feeling of mysticism hovers over the lovely PRIORY FARM of Frederick L. M. Griggs, whose decorative, almost formalized detail has had a pronounced effect upon younger British etchers, notably Tanner, Drury, Hoyton, and Sutherland. Tanner's MARTIN'S HOVEL on page 69 goes even Griggs one better in mysticism. But the dreaming Griggs also possessed a practical mastery of biting which the younger etchers cannot yet rival. One senses this fact in the sureness of DUNTISBOURNE ROUSE. The rich blacks which drypoint can achieve are demonstrated in the interior of the GREAT TITHE BARN by A. R. Middleton Todd. Shower and sunshine on the farm are graphically portrayed on page 73—Rushbury's COTSWOLD FARM cringing under glowering skies, in contrast to the sun-soaked haymaking scene photographed beneath it.

Rural England has many brilliant interpreters among British etchers, none of whom is more spontaneous than James McBey, whose SURREY DOWNS, a masterpiece of sensitive yet direct statement, opens the section on the English countryside. McBey's spectacular rise to the forefront of modern etchers must be attributed to his own originality, narrative skill, and uncanny gift of indication. Whistler may have influenced him, but he possesses a robustness which never belonged to that fastidious master. Sir Francis Seymour Haden, of course, is both restful and inspiring in his landscape plates. The sureness of his draftsmanship permitted him to needle an etching plate from nature at a single sitting. Such a plate is EGHAM LOCK, and A WATER MEADOW may well be another. Many authorities pronounce Haden's "Shere Mill Pond" and "Sunset in Ireland" two of the finest landscape plates ever made.

A capable tree study is furnished by Walter James, whose ROWAN ON THE HILLSIDE is rich and detailed. It is difficult to look upon the clear-cut plates by John Sell Cotman and realize that they were executed well over a century ago. His softground etchings, made with pencils and greatly resembling lithographs, might have been done yesterday. In his *Liber Studiorum*, an obvious emulation of Turner, he produced some of the most remarkable plates ever made by this process. His admiration for Piranesi may be detected in the bold virility of his own work. CADER IDRIS—NORTH WALES, a softground by this contemporary of Crome and Turner, looks no older than the contemporary lithograph on the same page, from a stone by Anthony R. Barker.

Frank Brangwyn, painter, muralist, illustrator, and etcher, has never been held down by the limitations of copper. His plates are usually massive and almost invariably dramatic, imbued with the artist's virile imagination and bold, free draftsmanship. Brangwyn seems to delight in contradicting Whistler's assertion that "the large plate is an abomination." His BLACK MILL, reduced many times for this reproduction, has been selected to prove the point. Bone's compositions are always breathtaking, a term which can certainly be applied to THE BALLANTRAE ROAD, on page 82. The feeling of immensity in this simple scene, the intangible sense of unseen things over the brow of the hill, is deeply moving. Bone achieved the same miracle in his famous "Ayr Prison" which, unfortunately, is not among these reproductions. The Canadian-American etcher, Kerr Eby, catches the same sense of limitless expanse in SALISBURY PLAINS. He has recorded the snowy landscapes of New England with equal skill. Another of his landscapes appears on page 92. Beatrice M. Christy proves that the hills and fields of rural England can be sympathetically interpreted in the medium of wood engraving in CHANCTONBURY RING. Malcolm Osborne, the present head of the Royal Society of Painter-Etchers and Engravers, and Sir Frank Short's successor as Principal of the Engraving School at the Royal College of Art, is celebrated for his portraits on copper and for his eloquent landscapes, of which AFTER THE STORM—AMBERLEY is one. The rugged Northumberland Coast has an equally faithful interpreter in Oliver Hall (page 85). Bouverie-Hoyton is again conscious of decorative form and texture in PLOVERS BARROW. Graham Sutherland's PECKEN WOOD has the same qualities, and is perhaps a trifle ominous. But SPRING, David Lucas' sprightly mezzotint, has all the romantic charm of the Constable painting which it reproduces. Sir Frank Short's rich, poetic COTTAGES AND HARVESTERS possesses the freshness of a watercolor, although there is no more slow or tedious medium than that of mezzotint, in which it was executed. The reverent Griggs can desert his beloved Gothic for pure landscape, as the sombre and lovely CROSS HANDS proves. The flat plains surrounding historic Ely provide a fruitful vantage point for etchers. Witness Stuart Brown's ELY; STORM COMING on page 88 or James McBey's THE ISLE OF ELY on page 153. There is a sense of boreboding, unfortunately well founded, in Bone's dramatic and overcast panorama of THE SOLENT. These shores in recent years have seen even blacker days. A more idyllic England, one which enjoyed a security not known in the days of dive bombers, is set down in Turner's SALWAY MOSS, interpreted in mezzotint by the versatile Sir Frank Short. The hand of time is set back also in Joseph Constantin Stadler's poetic color aquatint of ASHBURNHAM, which paints the wooded hills in tones of nostalgic beauty. Storm and midsummer calm are depicted on page 90, first by H. F. Waring's vigorous, wind-swept plate, NEAR CHICHESTER, and then by John Fullwood's sun-drenched etching of AN ENGLISH COMMON. J. M. W. Turner's own mezzotint of the JUNCTION OF THE SEVERN AND WYE proves that, given the time, he could have done all the mezzotint work on his own plates with consummate skill. Instead he turned most of the slow work over to professional assistants. Bouverie-Hoyton is in something of an overcast mood, but skillful as ever, in his etching of HIGH KNAPS. One feels the storm hovering over Badmin's SWINBROOK BRIDGE, an exquisite little plate which marks him as one of the most gifted exponents of the bitten line.

The recent death of the venerable Sir David Young Cameron has robbed Scotland of her pre-eminent spokesman in the graphic arts. From the time he began etching in 1887,

Cameron produced more than five hundred plates of architectural and landscape subjects. Of these, none is more admired than his majestic BEN LOMOND, long considered a superlative example of his work and, with BEN LEDI and THE FIVE SISTERS—YORK MINSTER (page 144), the most desirable "museum piece" in his long list of plates. THE HILLS OF TULLOCH, one of his more recent prints, is rich in Cameronesque blacks which contrast with the deft indication of mountains and foreground. Cameron achieves a sombre magnificence in BEN LEDI (page 104), a large and moving plate with no suspicion of cheer. His delicate sketch of GLENCAPLE ON THE NITH and the etching of DINNET MOOR are in a lighter vein. Joseph Gray is another native of Scotland well qualified to record the dour moods of its landscape. His PITMAN MOOR is certainly not a cheerful print, but how magnificently strong it is! Though Scotch mist is surely an elusive etching subject Gray has caught it with great skill in BADENOCH, on page 111. James McBey sees Scotland in a sunnier mood. He has imbued his delightful etching of THE MORAY FIRTH with humor, light, and imagination. One studies the children, the kites, the harbor and the sailboats disappearing into the horizon with nothing short of delight. McIntosh Patrick's clear-cut etching of KYLEAKIN is finely balanced, and he has achieved a silvery quality in his water which is rare in etching. Albany Howarth's spacious and romantic GOUROCK speaks highly of his technical ability but says little for the cheerfulness of the highland landscape.

England's vital arteries, her rivers, are also fertile sources of inspiration to her artists. William Walcot's sensitive plate, THE TYNE, is proof of the point. The silvery sheen of a calm river on a grey day has been subtly emphasized in the wiping of this plate. Rushbury's unusually large drypoint, ON THE WAVENAY, places more emphasis on the architecture than on the river. In WALBERSWICK FERRY—1914, Sir Muirhead Bone again achieves one of those tenuous compositions which would flounder in less competent hands. The path of interest in this drypoint is fascinating to follow. The little etching of PUTNEY CHURCH seems to catch the essence of a suburban village on the banks of the Thames. Sir Francis Seymour Haden's SAWLEY ABBEY is pure placidity, and very pure etching. His succeeding plate, FULHAM ON THE THAMES, was done for a French publisher, as a close examination of the lettering will show. Maxime Lalanne, beloved old French teacher of etching and author of one of the finest textbooks on the subject, was another of the small company of French artists who worked in England. His exquisite little etching of THE BANKS OF THE THAMES on Page 116 proves that he did not work in vain.

Norman Wilkinson, the favorite etcher of many sportsmen, catches the drama of fishing in swift-moving streams with sure, rapid strokes of his drypoint needle. One feels the steady pull of the current in SHEPHERDS POOL—ORCHY. Griggs, on the contrary, is serenity itself in his rendition of THE TRENT on the same page. There is little of the stylized Griggs in this plate, but a great deal of sincere landscape. Robert Havell's poetic color aquatint VIEW OF THE THAMES AT STREATLEY bears the fine stamp of the early nineteenth century, but John Sell Cotman's softground etching of MILLBANK ON THE THAMES might be a leaf from an artist's notebook in the year 1939, except for the archaic sails.

To introduce the coast of England, a young English pictorialist, Sidney Tushingham, makes his sole appearance. A Cornwall fishing village is rich subject matter for an etcher. Tushingham treats it tranquilly in CORNWALL, but James McBey interprets another mood in his famous GALE AT PORT ERROL on page 122, one of the greatest prints by the Scottish master who, incidentally, is now living in the United States. With utmost economy of line he has indicated the savage intensity of the tempest as it whips across the little port, buffeting the anxious group of villagers. The narrative quality is strong in this memorable plate, as it is in McBey's MERSEA; SUNSET. This extraordinary etching is perhaps the best example of the etcher's unique ability to depict the setting sun by a total blank spot on his copper. It almost hurts one's eyes to look directly at the center of this print. Martin Hardie achieves a like effect in SUNSET AT HEYBRIDGE on the same page. Bone's striking lithograph, READY FOR SEA, was one of a series he made during the first World War, and THE MYSTERY SHIP—PADSTOW, unusually rich in burr, is one of the least known of his drypoints. On the same page is Henry Rushbury's dramatic composition of a shipyard in Richborough, one of the most exposed ports on the Kentish coast. Haden's SUNSET ON THE THAMES is in distinct contrast to McBey's sunset at Mersea, but it is no less skillful and dramatic. The dexterous Francis Dodd proves in ANCHOR QUAY, I believe, that his mastery of drypoint is complete, and that his niche is very close to Bone's. Dodd's true forte, however, is portraiture. Some of the most remarkable portraits ever scratched with a needle on copper must be attributed to him.

A change of pace is afforded by Joseph Pennell's sketchy but satisfying little lithograph of THE PORT—NEWQUAY, one of the many joyful sketches in lithograph that he used to dash off during his travels in England. Turn the page and you encounter a print which probably took a hundred times as long to execute, the massive mezzotint by Sir Frank Short after Turner, VESSEL IN DISTRESS OFF YARMOUTH. This is an astounding print, one of the few great contemporary mezzotints, impressive not only for its dramatic intensity but for the complete technical mastery of the artist. Nothing could be more difficult to render on copper than a raging sea. Page 129 affords two interesting studies of the same little seaport of Mevagissey, in Cornwall. Kerr Eby, the etcher, has caught it in a cheerless rain storm. William McGreal, the photographer, has approached it from another point of view, and shows the village on a calm, sunny day.

England's castles provide her etchers with some of their most romantic subjects. This quality pervades Short's PEVERIL CASTLE, executed here in drypoint by this versatile master of many media. RICHMOND CASTLE by Percival Gaskell and KILCHURN CASTLE by Kenneth Steel possess a legendary, story book atmosphere. John Sell Cotman spent much time recording the picturesque castles of Wales in softground etching. His plates of CARNARVON, DOLBADARN and BAMBOROUGH CASTLES seem to be endowed with a timeless reality. Two widely contrasting views of Windsor Castle are presented on page 137. Twentieth-century aerial photography permits the inquisitive spectator to look behind the walls and see the rambling old castle as a whole, while Robert Havell's color aquatint gives him no more than a discreet glimpse of one of the wings. But Havell provides a recompense in his soft and gracious foreground. Sir Frank Short does full justice to the ruined KNARESBOROUGH CASTLE in his vigorous, painter-like mezzotint. Many of

Frederick L. M. Griggs' architectural subjects were the children of his mediaeval turn of mind. This may well be the case with THE MAYPOLE, which might be classified as midway between castle and manor. The drawing holds so closely to genuine Tudor forms that the subject has an atmosphere of absolute authenticity.

The final group of pictures in THIS REALM, THIS ENGLAND is devoted to its most inspiring monuments, its churches and cathedrals. Here again the eminent Gothicist Griggs has produced some of the greatest architectural plates. One is the courageous and unconventional ST. MARY'S—NOTTINGHAM, a composition which few artists would dare attempt. One of Sir D. Y. Cameron's unquestioned masterpieces, perhaps his greatest, follows on the next page. THE FIVE SISTERS, YORK MINSTER shows him in his full, sombre magnificence. No etcher has achieved more eloquent blacks. Frank Brangwyn's more animated nature has led to the finely balanced, almost rollicking vista of the CHURCH OF ST. WALBURG, a large plate printed in two tones of sepia. James McBey's versatility is evident in the tenebrous and serene manner in which he etches NIGHT IN ELY CATHEDRAL, an inspiring plate, full of fervor and dramatic contrast, which will help to make McBey's place secure among the great etchers. The noble mass of CANTERBURY CATHEDRAL, the most perilously exposed of all English cathedrals, has been finely recorded by H. Gordon Warlow, etcher of many ecclesiastical subjects in England. Warlow is a thorough mediaevalist, a fact which is best indicated by the Elizabethan figures which almost always grace his compositions. ST. BOTOLPH'S—BOSTON is one of Griggs' noblest plates, as it is one of his most daring compositions. Architecturally superb, the famed "Boston Stump" provides the etcher with a dramatic profile which he has recorded in a mood of sad and pensive loveliness. In ST. IPPOLYTS, Griggs is in a gayer mood, and not alone because of the frolicking lambs. Here he has accomplished something exceedingly rare in etching—the portrayal of sunlight through trees. In this plate he is looking directly into the sun, and the contre-jour effect of the silhouetted foliage is truly remarkable. Frederick Slocombe's twilight view of STRATFORD CHURCH is reminiscent of the large etchings which were in favor at the close of the nineteenth century. A complete

calm pervades this plate and its companion, Griggs' dreamy TATTERSHALL. The cathedral of Ely stands up equally well, seen from a distance by James McBey's appreciative eye, or close at hand by the camera, as a study of page 153 will show.

This collection of a few prints and photographs of England cannot, of course, paint a complete picture of the subject. But England's widely traveled etchers have drawn an eloquent, somewhat saddening and, let us hope, unforgettable sketch of this citadel of a valiant and triumphant race.

Samuel Chamberlain

THIS REALM, THIS ENGLAND . . .

List of Illustrations

RIVERS

THE COAST OF ENGLAND

Index by Artists

Acknowledgment

Grateful appreciation is expressed by the editor and the publisher to the etchers represented in this book, and to the following, who have kindly loaned prints from their collections for these reproductions:

THE LIBRARY OF CONGRESS, Washington, D. C.
THE METROPOLITAN MUSEUM OF ART, New York
THE NEW YORK PUBLIC LIBRARY
THE MUSEUM OF FINE ARTS, Boston
KENNEDY AND COMPANY, New York
HARLOW, KEPPEL AND COMPANY, New York
M. KNOEDLER AND COMPANY, New York
GOODSPEED'S BOOK SHOP, Boston
JOHN TAYLOR ARMS, Fairfield, Connecticut

The three prints by William Walcot are reproduced with the permission of his publishers, Messrs. A. C. and H. W. Dickens.

The photographs reproduced are from the collections of

BRITISH COMBINE PICTURES, New York
BRITISH LIBRARY OF INFORMATION, New York
EWING GALLOWAY, New York
WILLIAM McGREAL, Hancock, New Hampshire
G. L. HAWKINS, Culmstock, Devon, England

Pencil drawings by the editor are reproduced with the permission of the Architectural Book Publishing Co., New York.

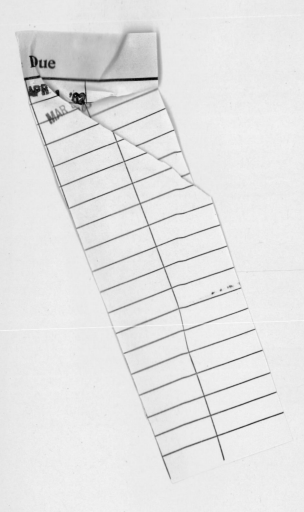

Due

APR 1 '82

MAR